DAVID A. ADLER'S
First Grade
MATH WORKBOOK

Illustrated by Edward Miller

HOLIDAY HOUSE · NEW YORK

Dear Parents and Teachers,

I'm a former math teacher and have been a published author for many years. I have happily combined my two careers in writing many introductory math books for young children. As a teacher, I knew that children need to not just learn basic math skills and concepts, but to practice them, and practice them again.

In this *First Grade Math Workbook*, artist Edward Miller and I used the common core curriculum and math standards for first grade to produce a workbook that makes learning and practicing simple math concepts clear and entertaining. This book gives young students a chance to practice adding and subtracting by tens, do simple equations, practice money basics and telling time, and develop their understanding of basic shapes.

Edward and I hope this book will provide enjoyment for young learners while they practice and learn, just as we have enjoyed bringing it to you.

Thank you,

David A. Adler

Contents

Addition and Subtraction

Add One More

Add an object to each group. Then count the objects and write the total number.

1 + 1 = 2

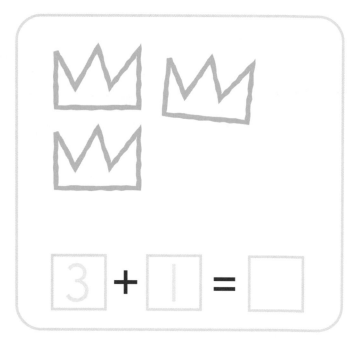

3 + 1 = ☐

2 + 1 = ☐

4 + 1 = ☐

Take One Away

Look at the objects in each box. Cross one out. How many are left? Don't count the one you crossed out.

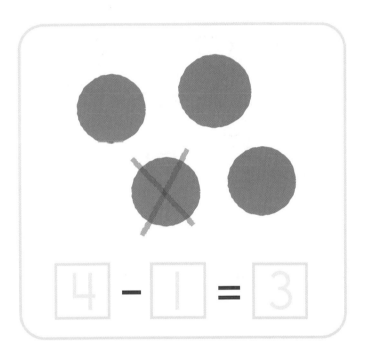

$4 - 1 = 3$

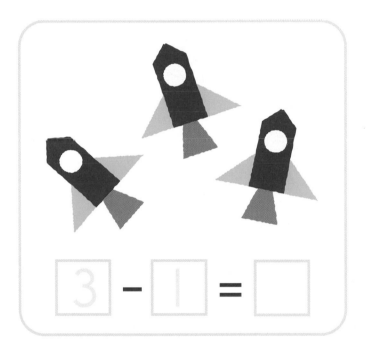

$3 - 1 = \boxed{}$

$6 - 1 = \boxed{}$

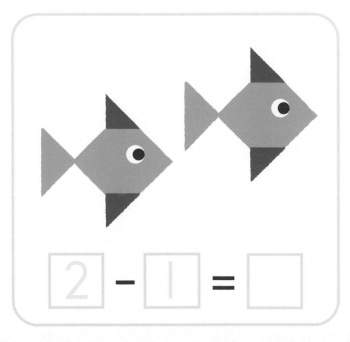

$2 - 1 = \boxed{}$

Add One More

Add an object to each group. Then count the objects and write the total number.

4 + 1 = 5

7 + 1 =

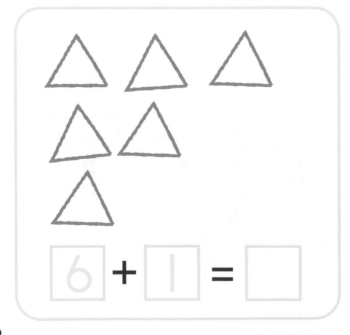

6 + 1 =

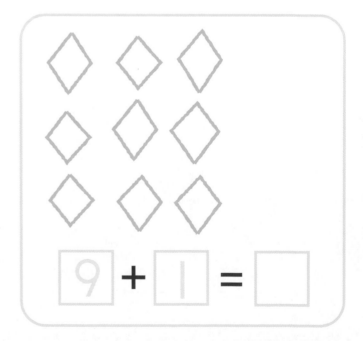

9 + 1 =

Take One Away

Look at the objects in each box. Cross one out.
How many are left? Don't count the one you
crossed out.

10 − 1 = 9

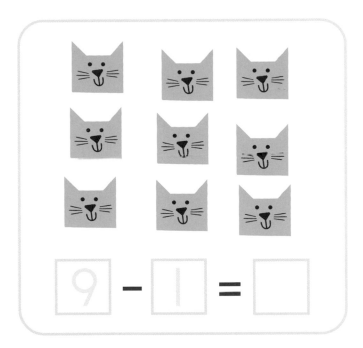

9 − 1 =

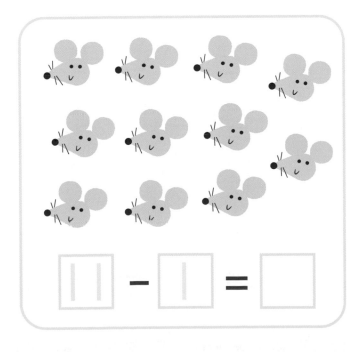

11 − 1 =

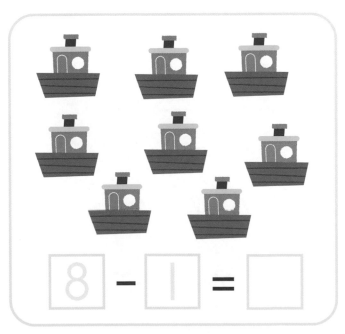

8 − 1 =

4

Add Two More

Add two objects to each group. Then count the objects and write the total number.

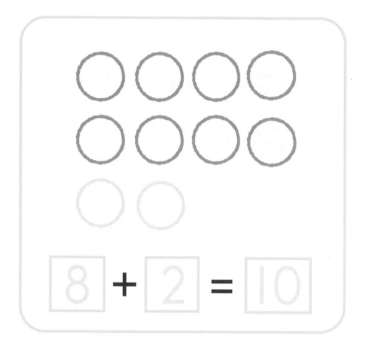

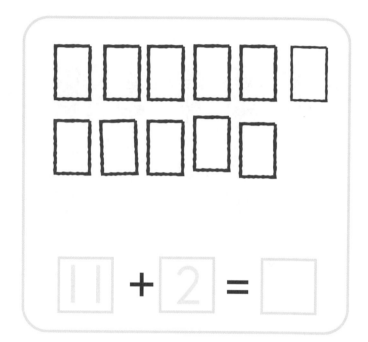

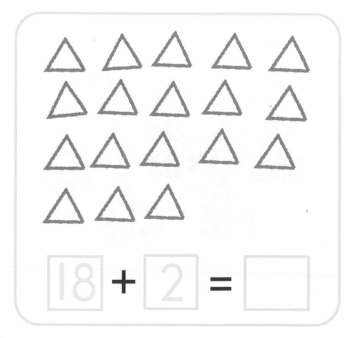

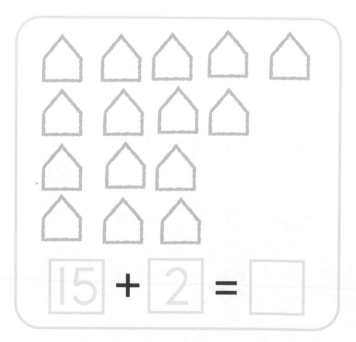

Take Two Away

Look at the objects in each box. Cross two out. How many are left? Don't count the two you crossed out.

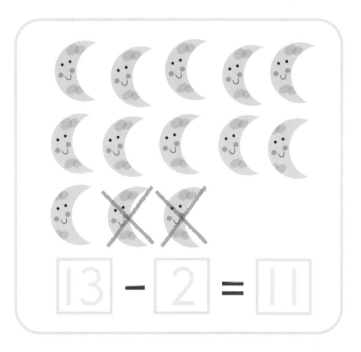

13 – 2 = 11

20 – 2 =

18 – 2 =

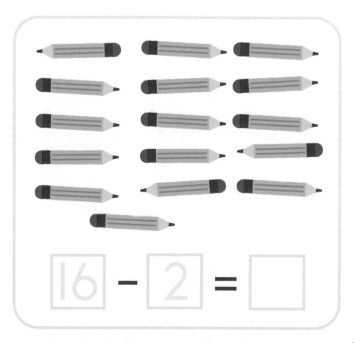

16 – 2 =

Practice adding and subtracting.

4 + 3 = ☐7

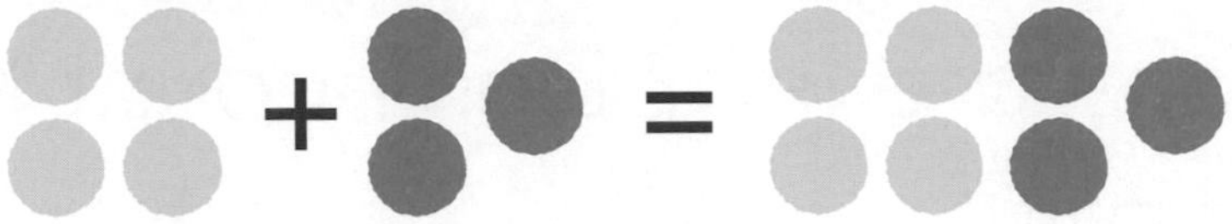

3 + 6 = ☐9

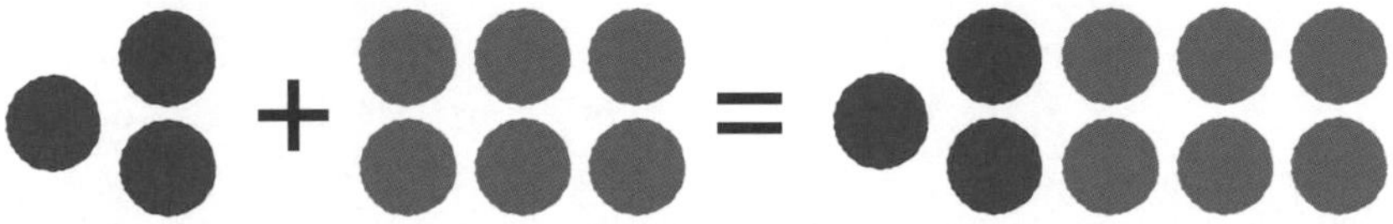

2 + 4 = ☐

9 + 5 = ☐

4 + 4 + 3 = ☐

2 + 5 + 8 = ☐

12 + 2 = ☐

11 + 4 = ☐

15 + 5 = ☐

10 − 5 = 5

8 − 3 = 5

7 − 1 =

11 − 4 =

15 − 2 =

6 − 2 − 2 =

20 − 4 =

17 − 3 =

16 − 3 =

10 − 2 − 2 =

Here are some equations that show that there are many ways to add numbers

$$4 + 1 = 2 + 3$$

$$5 + 2 = 6 + 1$$

$$9 + 1 = 2 + 8$$

$$10 + 4 = 11 + 3$$

$$6 + 8 = 5 + 9$$

Fill in the missing number in each equation

$$2 + 2 = 3 + \boxed{1}$$

$$4 + 3 = 2 + \boxed{}$$

$$8 + 2 = 9 + \boxed{}$$

$$9 + 4 = 7 + \boxed{}$$

$$11 + 3 = 6 + \boxed{}$$

$$14 + 5 = 10 + \boxed{}$$

Understanding the Equal Sign

Circle the equations that are true,
cross out the equations that are false.

$$6 = 6$$

$$2 + 2 = 5$$

$$7 = 8 - 1$$

$$5 + 2 = 2 + 5$$

$$4 + 1 = 5 + 2$$

equal sign

$$4 + 3 = 6 + 1$$

$$8 + 2 = 10$$

$$7 + 3 = 4 + 6$$

$$10 + 9 = 20$$

$$11 + 3 = 14$$

What number is missing in these problems?

8 + ☐3 = 11

5 = ☐ − 3

6 + 6 = 2 + ☐

4 + ☐ = 6

2 + 4 + ☐ = 12

13 + □ = 19

10 + □ = 11 + 3

□ + 8 = 5 + 9

20 = 9 + □

14

The spaceship has 5 passengers and 2 pilots.
How many people are in the spaceship?

2 + 5 = 7

There are 5 big dogs and 9 small dogs in
the neighborhood. How many dogs are in
the neighborhood all together?

☐ + ☐ = ☐

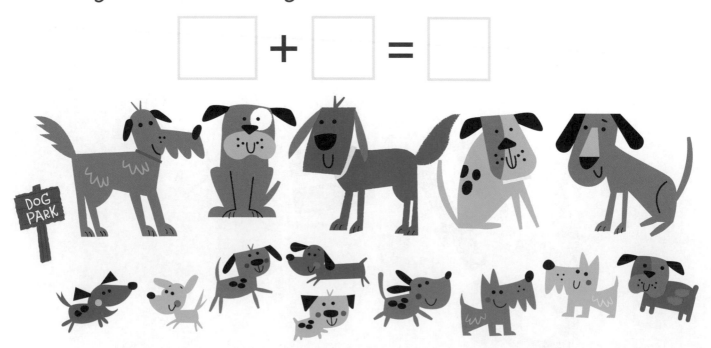

DOG PARK

There were 11 bats in the haunted house.
5 bats flew away. How many bats are left
in the haunted house?

Sarah had 20 marbles. She lost 3.
How many marbles does Sarah have left?

16

The pumpkin patch had 18 pumpkins. We brought 6 pumpkins home. How many pumpkins are left in the patch?

☐ − ☐ = ☐

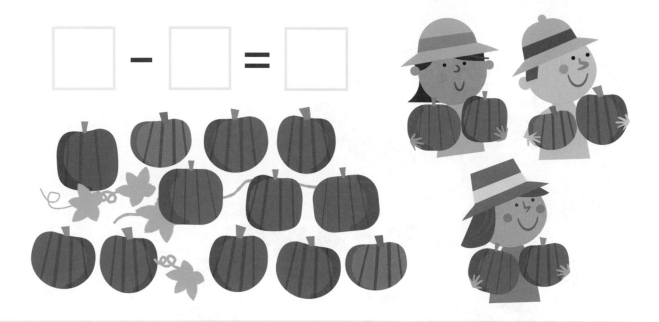

Ed had 15 pieces of candy. He gave 4 to Jane. How many pieces of candy does he have now?

☐ − ☐ = ☐

Then he ate 3 pieces. How many pieces of candy does he have left?

☐ − ☐ = ☐

Danielle saw a haunted house with skeletons in the windows! There were 4 windows in the house, and each window had 2 skeletons. How many skeletons were there?

☐ + ☐ + ☐ + ☐ = ☐

Billy's mother gave him 10 pennies to buy a lollipop. The lollipop cost 6 cents. After he bought the lollipop, how many pennies did Billy have left?

☐ − ☐ = ☐

Counting to 120

Here is a grid that shows how to count from 1 to 120

1	2	3	4	5	6	7	8	9	10
11	12	13	14	15	16	17	8	19	20
21	22	23	24	25	26	27	28	29	30
31	32	33	34	35	36	37	38	39	40
41	42	43	44	45	46	47	48	49	50
51	52	53	54	55	56	57	58	59	60
61	62	63	64	65	66	67	68	69	70
71	72	73	74	75	76	77	78	79	80
81	82	83	84	85	86	87	88	89	90
91	92	93	94	95	96	97	98	99	100
101	102	103	104	105	106	107	108	109	110
111	112	113	114	115	116	117	118	119	120

Count to 120. Fill in the missing numbers.

1	2	3	4	5		7		9	
11	12	13	14		16	17	18		20
21	22	23		25		27	28	29	30
31		33	34	35	36		38	39	
	42	43	44		46	47	48	49	50
		53	54		56		58	59	
61	62	63		65	66	67		69	70
	72	73	74		76		78	79	
81	82		84		86		88		90
91	92		94	95			98	99	100
101	102	103		105	106	107	108		
	112		114	115			118	119	120

Counting by 10s

Count to 120 by 10s.

●●●●●●●●●	10	one ten
●●●●●●●●●	20	two tens
●●●●●●●●●	30	three tens
●●●●●●●●●	40	four tens
●●●●●●●●●	50	five tens
●●●●●●●●●	60	six tens
●●●●●●●●●	70	seven tens
●●●●●●●●●	80	eight tens
●●●●●●●●●	90	nine tens
●●●●●●●●●	100	ten tens
●●●●●●●●●	110	eleven tens
●●●●●●●●●	120	twelve tens

How Many 10s?

Write the number of tens in the
first box, and the total number
of dots in the second box.

one 10

10

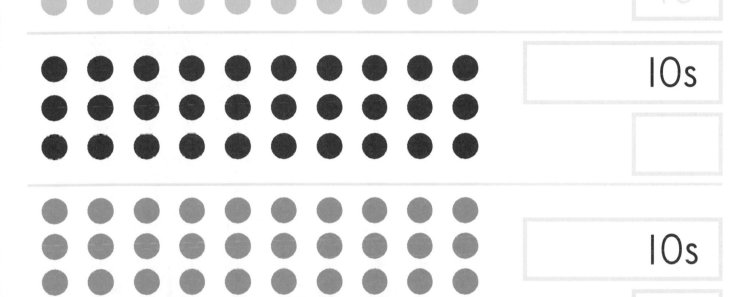

10s

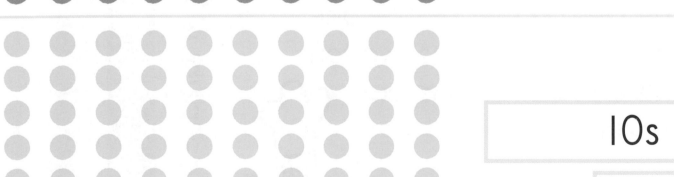

10s

10s

We write numbers with digits.

The order of the digits is important.

216 and **621** have the same digits, but because their order is different, the numbers are different.

The **6** in 21**6** means six ones.
The **1** in 2**1**6 means one ten.
The **2** in **2**16 means two hundreds.

Hundreds Tens Ones

2 1 6

The **1** in 62**1** means one one.
The **2** in 6**2**1 means two tens.
The **6** in **6**21 means six hundreds.

Hundreds Tens Ones

6 2 1

Circle the correct number
in each problem below.

1. Circle the digit that shows
how many 10s there are.

4 1 3

2. Circle the digit that shows
how many 10s there are.

5 2

3. Circle the digit that shows
how many 100s there are.

3 2 1

4. Circle the digit that shows
how many 10s there are.

2 3

5. Circle the digit that shows
how many 1s there are.

7 6

6. Circle the digit that shows
how many 100s there are.

8 0 0

A penny  = 1¢

A dime  = 10¢

A nickel  = 5¢

A quarter = 25¢

Five pennies are equal to a nickel.

     =

Two nickels are equal to a dime.

 =

Two dimes and a nickel are equal to a quarter.

Two dimes and five pennies are also equal to a quarter.

One dime, two nickels, and five pennies are also equal to a quarter.

26

Circle five pennies. How much money is this?

1¢ + 1¢ + 1¢ + 1¢ + 1¢ =

5¢

Circle four nickels. How much money is this?

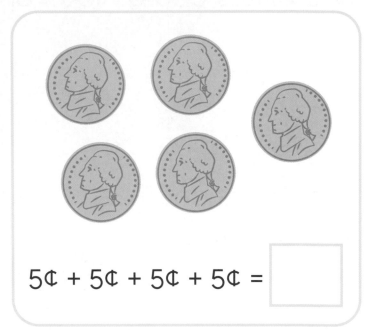

5¢ + 5¢ + 5¢ + 5¢ =

Circle three dimes. How much money is this?

10¢ + 10¢ + 10¢ =

Circle two quarters. How much money is this?

25¢ + 25¢ =

How much money is in each box?

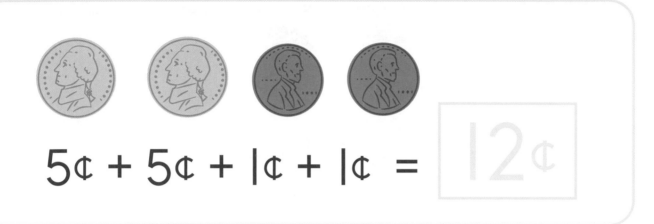

$$5¢ + 5¢ + 1¢ + 1¢ = \boxed{12¢}$$

$$10¢ + 10¢ + 10¢ + 5¢ = \boxed{}$$

I'm George Washington. I was the first president of the U.S.

Your portrait is on the quarter.

How much money is in each box?

25¢ + 25¢ + 1¢ =

10¢ + 10¢ + 5¢ + 1¢ =

25¢ + 10¢ + 10¢ + 5¢ =

25¢ + 25¢ + 10¢ + 5¢ + 1¢ =

    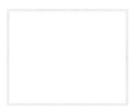

25¢ + 10¢ + 10¢ + 5¢ + 1¢ =

I am Abraham Lincoln. I was the 16th U.S. president. My portrait is on the penny and the 5-dollar bill.

I am Thomas Jefferson. I was the 3rd U.S. president. My portrait is on the nickel. I wrote the Declaration of Independence.

I am Franklin D. Roosevelt. I was the 32nd U.S. president. My portrait is on the dime.

More Than Ten, Less Than Ten

How many are here? Is the number in each group *more* than ten or *less* than ten? Circle the correct answer. Write down the number of items.

more than ten

less than ten

total items

more than ten

less than ten

total items

more than ten

less than ten

total items

Here are 3 circles. Add ten more.
How many do you have?

$$3 + 10 = \boxed{13}$$

Here are 5 triangles. Add ten more.
How many do you have?

$$5 + 10 = \boxed{}$$

Here are 18 hearts. Cross out ten of them.
How many are left? Remember, don't count
the ones you crossed out.

$$18 - 10 = \boxed{}$$

Adding Tens.
Practice adding tens.

8 + 10 = ☐18☐

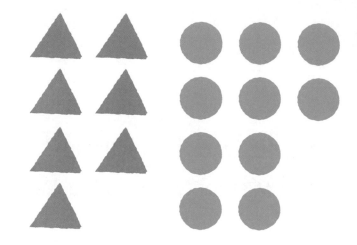

7 + 10 = ☐

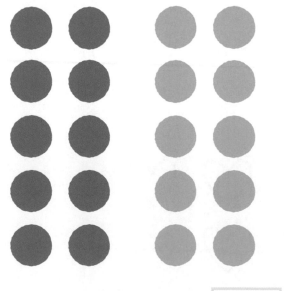

10 + 10 = ☐

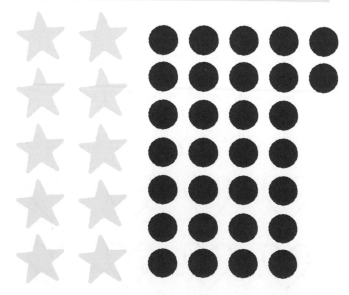

10 + 30 = ☐

Subtracting from Tens.

Practice subtracting from tens.

10 – 8 = ☐ 2

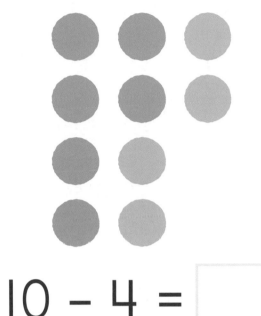

10 – 4 = ☐

20 – 12 = ☐

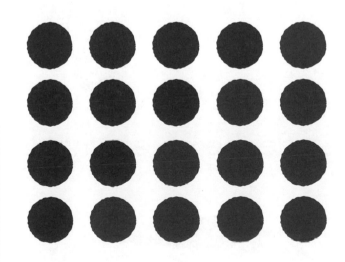

20 – 10 = ☐

Learn the words that compare length.

This bug is **short**.   This bug is **long**.

Now, compare length. Circle the object that is longest.

Circle the object that is shortest.

Which is shortest? Circle it.

Which is longest? Circle it.

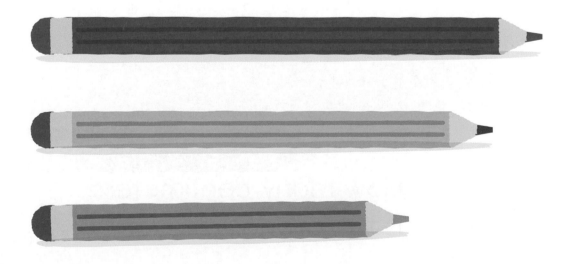

Here is a ruler.

Each number marks one inch.

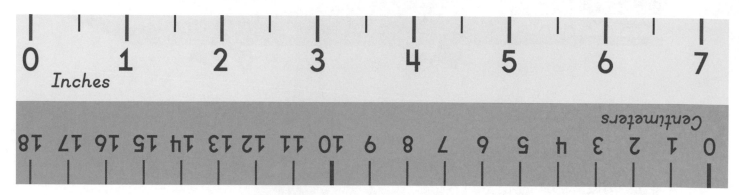

Turn the ruler upside down, and each number marks one centimeter.

How many inches is the blue crayon?

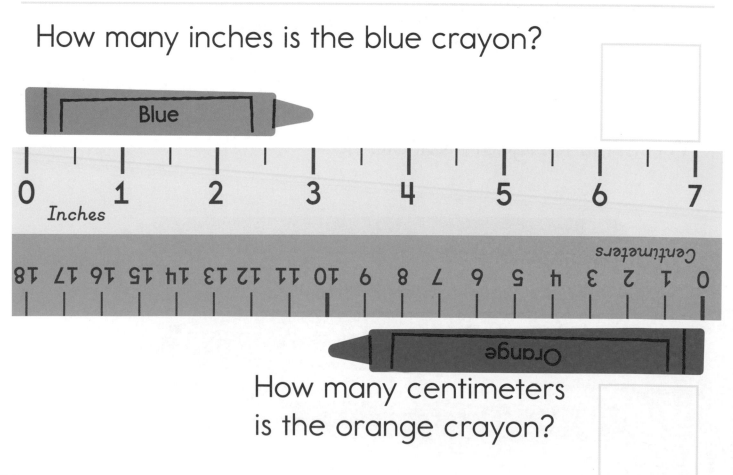

How many centimeters is the orange crayon?

How many inches is the red pencil?

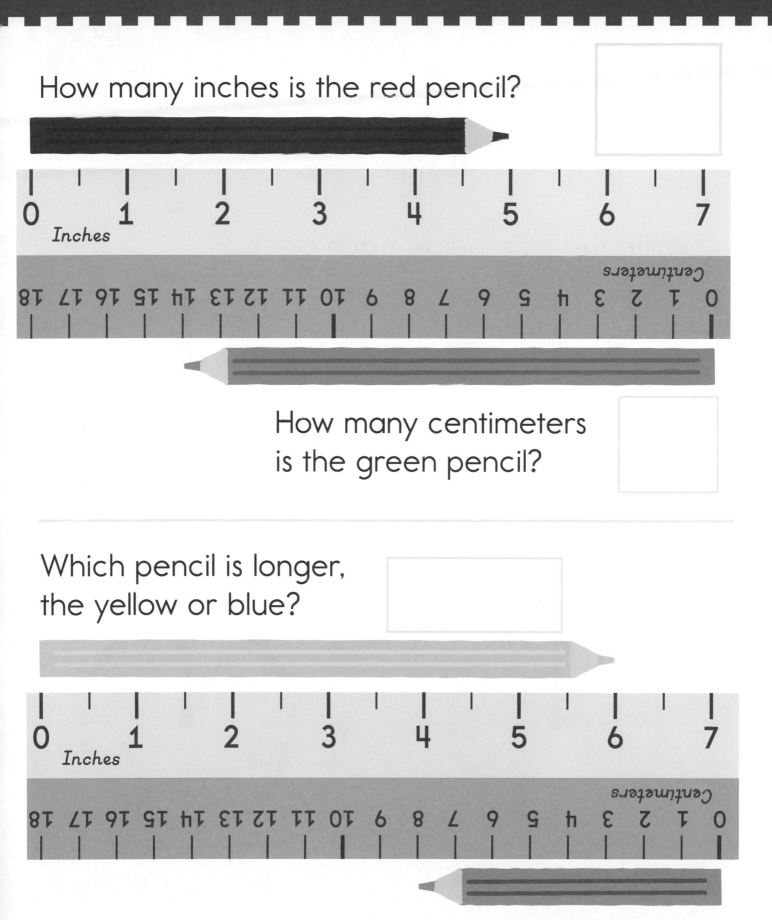

How many centimeters is the green pencil?

Which pencil is longer, the yellow or blue?

What time is it?

When the big hand is at 12,
it is always something o'clock.

Write the time below each clock.

It is [4] o'clock.

It is [ ] o'clock.

It is [ ] o'clock.

It is [ ] o'clock.

Draw the hands on the clock that show the correct time.

It is 1 o'clock.

It is 12 o'clock.

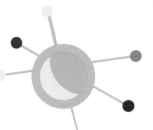

It is 3 o'clock.

It is 9 o'clock.

It is 7 o'clock.

On a digital clock, the time is shown in numbers.

When it is 3 o'clock, it looks like this on a digital clock:

analog clock   digital clock

Write the time on the analog clock onto the digital clock.

When the big hand is on the 6, it means it is **30 minutes** past the hour. For instance, this clock is 30 minutes past 3, or 3:30.

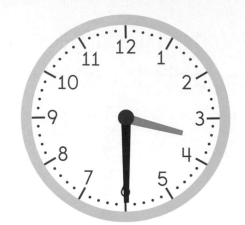

What time is it on these clocks? Write the time below.

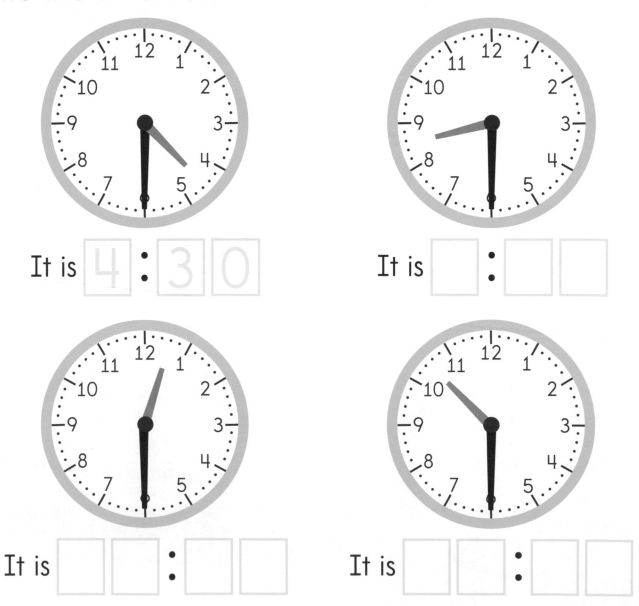

It is 4 : 30

It is ☐ : ☐☐

It is ☐☐ : ☐☐

It is ☐☐ : ☐☐

This is the time Amy leaves for the school bus. What time is it?

It is ☐ : ☐☐

This is the time that baby Owen takes his nap. What time is it?

It is ☐ : ☐☐

Ezra and Carmen have dinner at 6 o'clock. Show the time on both the clocks.

Represent and Interpret Data

Here are apples we picked for pie.

Red apples

Green apples

Half apples

Apples with no stems

How many apples don't have stems?

Which kind of apples are the same in number?

Which apples are there most of?

On the way home, we ate three apples!
How many apples did we have left for pie?

My grandmother loves birds.

How many birds does she have? □

How many birds have red beaks? □

How many birds are blue? □

How many more green birds
are there than yellow birds? □

Two birds flew away.
How many birds are left? □

What makes a shape a shape?

A **square** has four sides that are each the same length and four angles that are each the same.

A **rectangle** has four sides. Each pair of opposites sides are the same length and each of the four angles are the same.

A **triangle** has three sides.

A **circle** is round.

An **oval** is shaped like an egg.

Color the squares blue.
Color the triangles red.
Color the ovals yellow.

Color the rectangles orange.
Color the circles green.

Draw three shapes and write their names underneath.

Draw a line from each object on
the left to its shape on the right.

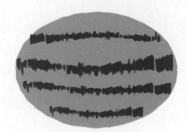

How many sides and corners
does each shape have?

sides ☐

corners ☐

sides ☐

corners ☐

sides ☐

corners ☐

sides ☐

corners ☐

sides ☐

corners ☐

sides ☐

corners ☐

Count the circles, rectangles, and triangles in this green-faced monster.

_____ circles

_____ rectangles

_____ triangles

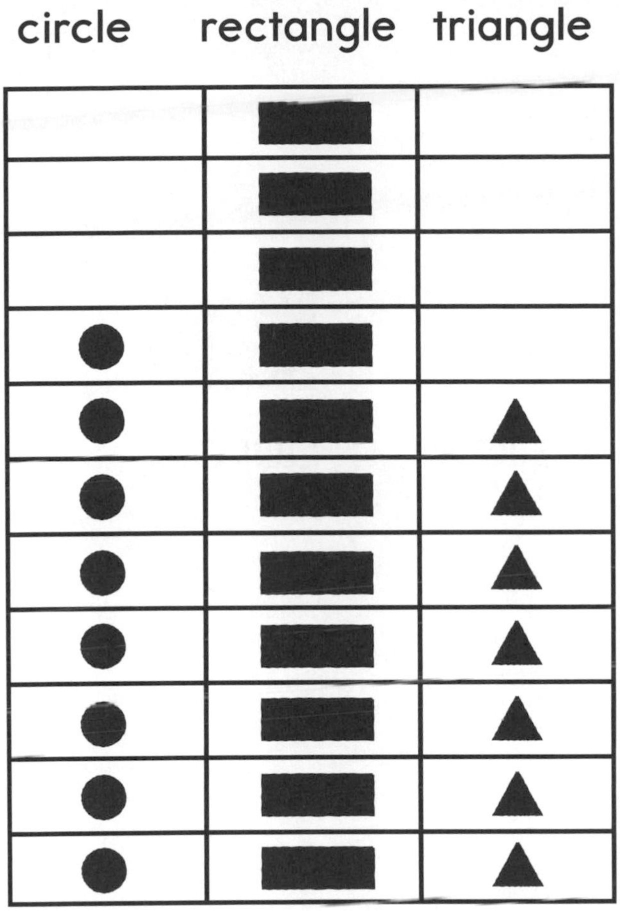

Represent and Interpret Data

circle	rectangle	triangle
	■	
	■	
	■	
●	■	
●	■	▲
●	■	▲
●	■	▲
●	■	▲
●	■	▲
●	■	▲
●	■	▲

This chart shows all the shapes that make up the green-faced monster. Look at the chart. Is the monster made of more circles or more triangles?

_____

How many more circles are there than triangles?

_____

Which has the highest number of shapes? _____

Which has the lowest number of shapes? _____

Shapes Search

Find the shapes in the picture!
Use the key to color the shapes

blue   orange   yellow   purple

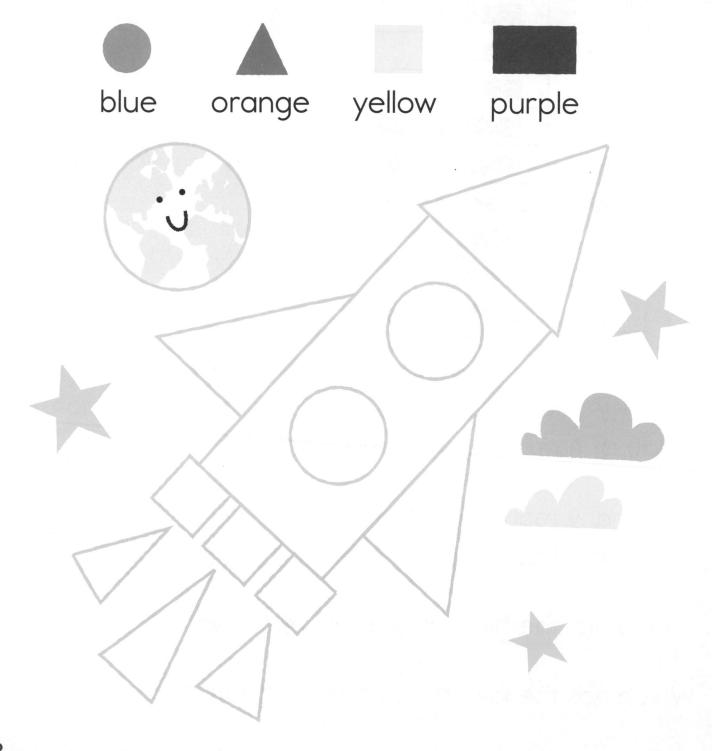

53

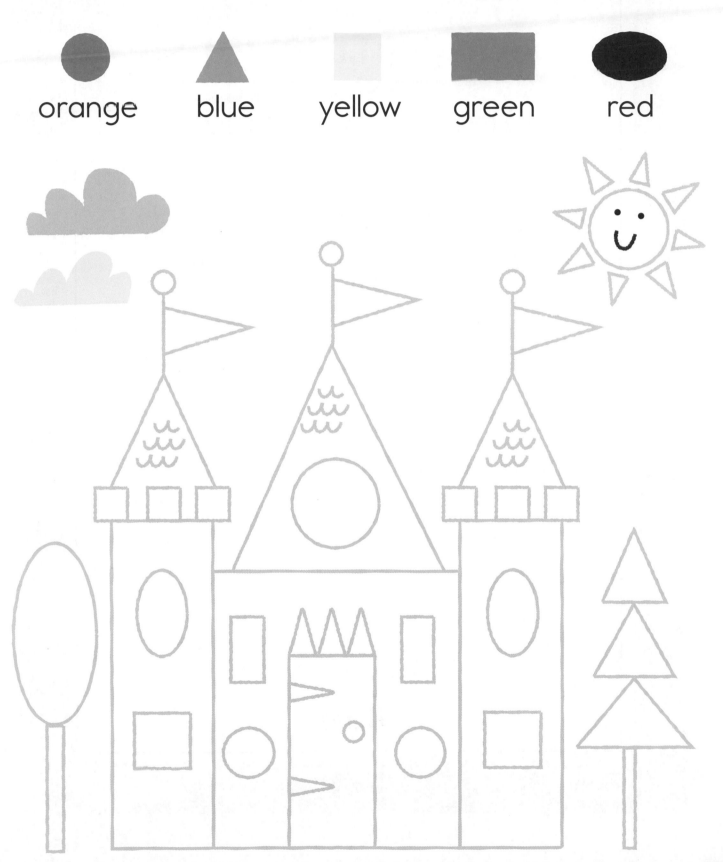

orange   blue   yellow   green   red

Congratulations!

You know all about place value and shapes. You've practiced telling time and adding and subtracting money. You can do word problems.

Good work!

_____
Name

_____
Date

page 1

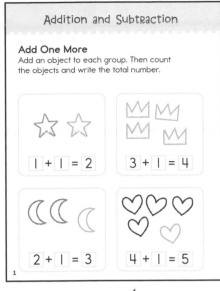

Addition and Subtraction

Add One More
Add an object to each group. Then count the objects and write the total number.

$1 + 1 = 2$ $3 + 1 = 4$

$2 + 1 = 3$ $4 + 1 = 5$

page 2

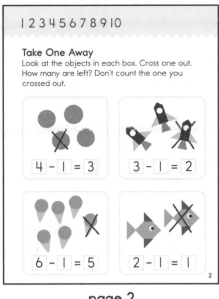

1 2 3 4 5 6 7 8 9 10

Take One Away
Look at the objects in each box. Cross one out. How many are left? Don't count the one you crossed out.

$4 - 1 = 3$ $3 - 1 = 2$

$6 - 1 = 5$ $2 - 1 = 1$

page 3

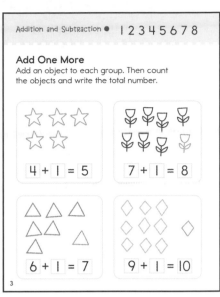

Addition and Subtraction ● 1 2 3 4 5 6 7 8

Add One More
Add an object to each group. Then count the objects and write the total number.

$4 + 1 = 5$ $7 + 1 = 8$

$6 + 1 = 7$ $9 + 1 = 10$

page 4

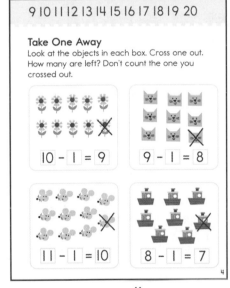

9 10 11 12 13 14 15 16 17 18 19 20

Take One Away
Look at the objects in each box. Cross one out. How many are left? Don't count the one you crossed out.

$10 - 1 = 9$ $9 - 1 = 8$

$11 - 1 = 10$ $8 - 1 = 7$

page 5

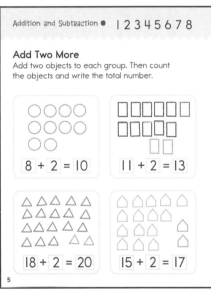

Addition and Subtraction ● 1 2 3 4 5 6 7 8

Add Two More
Add two objects to each group. Then count the objects and write the total number.

$8 + 2 = 10$ $11 + 2 = 13$

$18 + 2 = 20$ $15 + 2 = 17$

page 6

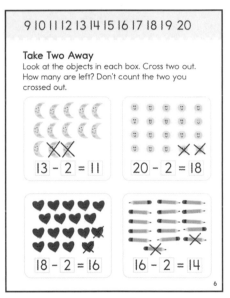

9 10 11 12 13 14 15 16 17 18 19 20

Take Two Away
Look at the objects in each box. Cross two out. How many are left? Don't count the two you crossed out.

$13 - 2 = 11$ $20 - 2 = 18$

$18 - 2 = 16$ $16 - 2 = 14$

page 7

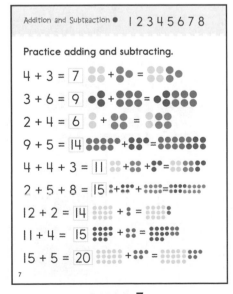

Addition and Subtraction ● 1 2 3 4 5 6 7 8

Practice adding and subtracting.

$4 + 3 = 7$
$3 + 6 = 9$
$2 + 4 = 6$
$9 + 5 = 14$
$4 + 4 + 3 = 11$
$2 + 5 + 8 = 15$
$12 + 2 = 14$
$11 + 4 = 15$
$15 + 5 = 20$

page 8

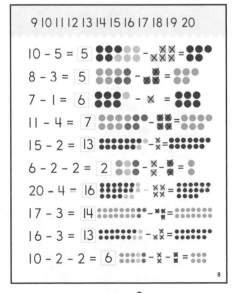

9 10 11 12 13 14 15 16 17 18 19 20

$10 - 5 = 5$
$8 - 3 = 5$
$7 - 1 = 6$
$11 - 4 = 7$
$15 - 2 = 13$
$6 - 2 - 2 = 2$
$20 - 4 = 16$
$17 - 3 = 14$
$16 - 3 = 13$
$10 - 2 - 2 = 6$

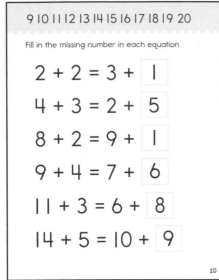

9 10 11 12 13 14 15 16 17 18 19 20

Fill in the missing number in each equation

$2 + 2 = 3 + \boxed{1}$

$4 + 3 = 2 + \boxed{5}$

$8 + 2 = 9 + \boxed{1}$

$9 + 4 = 7 + \boxed{6}$

$11 + 3 = 6 + \boxed{8}$

$14 + 5 = 10 + \boxed{9}$

10

page 10

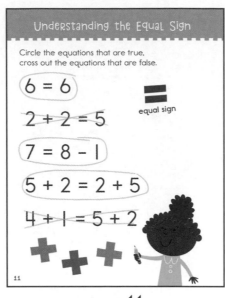

Understanding the Equal Sign

Circle the equations that are true,
cross out the equations that are false.

$\boxed{6 = 6}$

~~$2 + 2 = 5$~~

$\boxed{7 = 8 - 1}$

$\boxed{5 + 2 = 2 + 5}$

~~$4 + 1 = 5 + 2$~~

equal sign

11

page 11

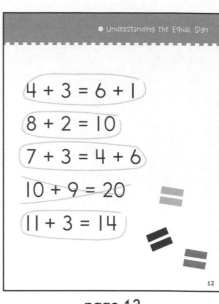

● Understanding the Equal Sign

$\boxed{4 + 3 = 6 + 1}$

$\boxed{8 + 2 = 10}$

$\boxed{7 + 3 = 4 + 6}$

~~$10 + 9 = 20$~~

$\boxed{11 + 3 = 14}$

12

page 12

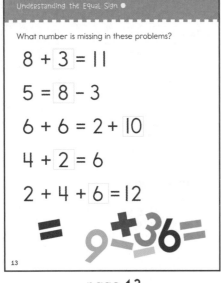

Understanding the Equal Sign ●

What number is missing in these problems?

$8 + \boxed{3} = 11$

$5 = 8 - \boxed{3}$

$6 + 6 = 2 + \boxed{10}$

$4 + 2 = \boxed{6}$

$2 + 4 + \boxed{6} = 12$

13

page 13

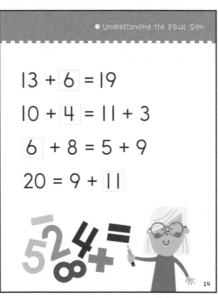

● Understanding the Equal Sign

$13 + 6 = \boxed{19}$

$10 + \boxed{4} = 11 + 3$

$\boxed{6} + 8 = 5 + 9$

$20 = 9 + \boxed{11}$

14

page 14

Word Problems

The spaceship has 5 passengers and 2 pilots.
How many people are in the spaceship?

$2 + 5 = \boxed{7}$

There are 5 big dogs and 9 small dogs in
the neighborhood. How many dogs are in
the neighborhood all together?

$5 + 9 = \boxed{14}$

15

page 15

● Word Problems

There were 11 bats in the haunted house.
5 bats flew away. How many bats are left
in the haunted house?

$11 - 5 = \boxed{6}$

Sarah had 20 marbles. She lost 3.
How many marbles does Sarah have left?

$20 - 3 = \boxed{17}$

16

page 16

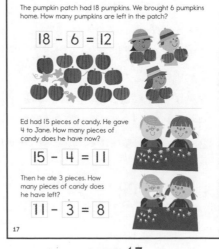

Word Problems ●

The pumpkin patch had 18 pumpkins. We brought 6 pumpkins
home. How many pumpkins are left in the patch?

$18 - 6 = \boxed{12}$

Ed had 15 pieces of candy. He gave
4 to Jane. How many pieces of
candy does he have now?

$15 - 4 = \boxed{11}$

Then he ate 3 pieces. How
many pieces of candy does
he have left?

$11 - 3 = \boxed{8}$

17

page 17

57

page 18

Danielle saw a haunted house with skeletons in the windows! There were 4 windows in the house, and each window had 2 skeletons. How many skeletons were there?

$$2 + 2 + 2 + 2 = 8$$

Billy's mother gave him 10 pennies to buy a lollipop. The lollipop cost 6 cents. After he bought the lollipop, how many pennies did Billy have left?

$$10 - 6 = 4$$

18

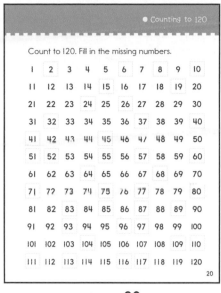

page 20

Count to 120. Fill in the missing numbers.

1	2	3	4	5	6	7	8	9	10
11	12	13	14	15	16	17	18	19	20
21	22	23	24	25	26	27	28	29	30
31	32	33	34	35	36	37	38	39	40
41	42	43	44	45	46	47	48	49	50
51	52	53	54	55	56	57	58	59	60
61	62	63	64	65	66	67	68	69	70
71	72	73	74	75	76	77	78	79	80
81	82	83	84	85	86	87	88	89	90
91	92	93	94	95	96	97	98	99	100
101	102	103	104	105	106	107	108	109	110
111	112	113	114	115	116	117	118	119	120

20

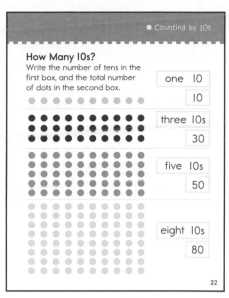

page 22

How Many 10s?
Write the number of tens in the first box, and the total number of dots in the second box.

one	10
	10

three 10s
30

five 10s
50

eight 10s
80

22

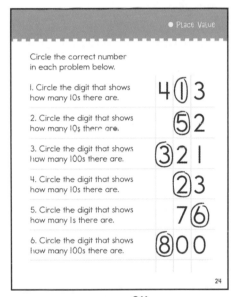

page 24

Circle the correct number in each problem below.

1. Circle the digit that shows how many 10s there are. 4 ①3

2. Circle the digit that shows how many 10s there are. ⑤2

3. Circle the digit that shows how many 100s there are. ③21

4. Circle the digit that shows how many 10s there are. ②3

5. Circle the digit that shows how many 1s there are. 7⑥

6. Circle the digit that shows how many 100s there are. ⑧00

24

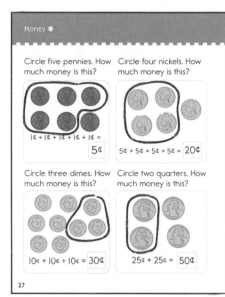

page 27

Circle five pennies. How much money is this?

$$1¢ + 1¢ + 1¢ + 1¢ + 1¢ = 5¢$$

Circle four nickels. How much money is this?

$$5¢ + 5¢ + 5¢ + 5¢ = 20¢$$

Circle three dimes. How much money is this?

$$10¢ + 10¢ + 10¢ = 30¢$$

Circle two quarters. How much money is this?

$$25¢ + 25¢ = 50¢$$

27

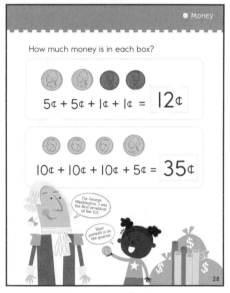

page 28

How much money is in each box?

$$5¢ + 5¢ + 1¢ + 1¢ = 12¢$$

$$10¢ + 10¢ + 10¢ + 5¢ = 35¢$$

28

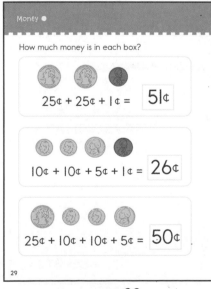

page 29

How much money is in each box?

$$25¢ + 25¢ + 1¢ = 51¢$$

$$10¢ + 10¢ + 5¢ + 1¢ = 26¢$$

$$25¢ + 10¢ + 10¢ + 5¢ = 50¢$$

29

page 30

$$25¢ + 25¢ + 10¢ + 5¢ + 1¢ = 66¢$$

$$25¢ + 10¢ + 10¢ + 5¢ + 1¢ = 51¢$$

30

58

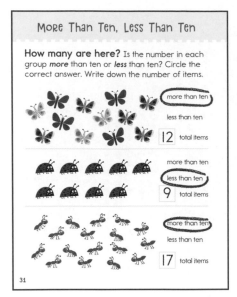

More Than Ten, Less Than Ten

How many are here? Is the number in each group *more* than ten or *less* than ten? Circle the correct answer. Write down the number of items.

(more than ten)
less than ten
12 total items

more than ten
(less than ten)
9 total items

(more than ten)
less than ten
17 total items

31

page 31

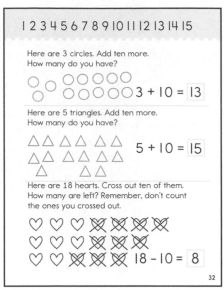

Here are 3 circles. Add ten more. How many do you have?

$3 + 10 = 13$

Here are 5 triangles. Add ten more. How many do you have?

$5 + 10 = 15$

Here are 18 hearts. Cross out ten of them. How many are left? Remember, don't count the ones you crossed out.

$18 - 10 = 8$

32

page 32

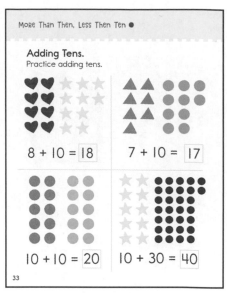

Adding Tens.
Practice adding tens.

$8 + 10 = 18$

$7 + 10 = 17$

$10 + 10 = 20$

$10 + 30 = 40$

33

page 33

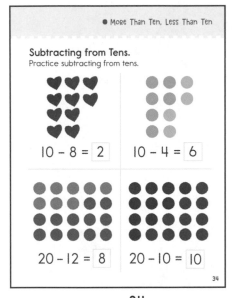

Subtracting from Tens.
Practice subtracting from tens.

$10 - 8 = 2$

$10 - 4 = 6$

$20 - 12 = 8$

$20 - 10 = 10$

34

page 34

Measuring

Learn the words that compare length.

This bug is **short**.   This bug is **long**.

Now, compare length. Circle the object that is longest.

Circle the object that is shortest.

35

page 35

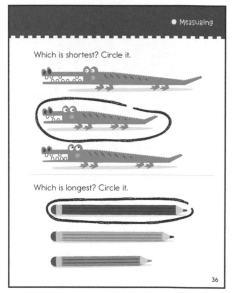

Which is shortest? Circle it.

Which is longest? Circle it.

36

page 36

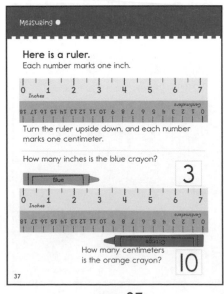

Here is a ruler.
Each number marks one inch.

Turn the ruler upside down, and each number marks one centimeter.

How many inches is the blue crayon?

3

How many centimeters is the orange crayon?

10

37

page 37

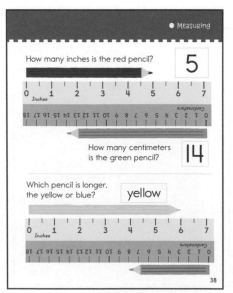

How many inches is the red pencil?

5

How many centimeters is the green pencil?

14

Which pencil is longer, the yellow or blue?

yellow

38

page 38

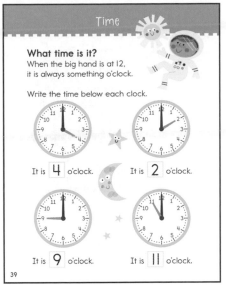

page 39

Time

What time is it?
When the big hand is at 12, it is always something o'clock.

Write the time below each clock.

It is **4** o'clock.   It is **2** o'clock.

It is **9** o'clock.   It is **11** o'clock.

39

page 40

● Time

Draw the hands on the clock that show the correct time.

It is 12 o'clock.

It is 1 o'clock.

It is 3 o'clock.

It is 9 o'clock.

It is 7 o'clock.

40

page 42

● Time

Write the time on the analog clock onto the digital clock.

5:00

8:00

11:00

42

page 43

Time ●

When the big hand is on the 6, it means it is **30 minutes** past the hour. For instance, this clock is 30 minutes past 3, or 3:30.

What time is it on these clocks? Write the time below.

It is **4:30**   It is **8:30**

It is **12:30**   It is **10:30**

43

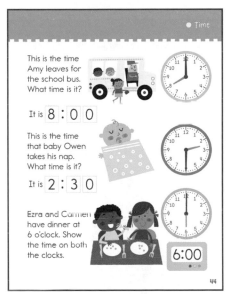

page 44

● Time

This is the time Amy leaves for the school bus. What time is it?

It is **8:00**

This is the time that baby Owen takes his nap. What time is it?

It is **2:30**

Ezra and Carmen have dinner at 6 o'clock. Show the time on both the clocks.

6:00

44

page 45

Represent and Interpret Data

Here are apples we picked for pie.

Red apples

Green apples

Half apples

Apples with no stems

How many apples don't have stems?   **4**

Which kind of apples are the same in number?
green apples and apple without stems

Which apples are there most of?   **red apples**

On the way home, we ate three apples! How many apples did we have left for pie?   **13**

45

page 46

● Represent and Interpret Data

My grandmother loves birds.

How many birds does she have?   **12**

How many birds have red beaks?   **2**

How many birds are blue?   **5**

How many more green birds are there than yellow birds?   **1**

Two birds flew away. How many birds are left?   **10**

46

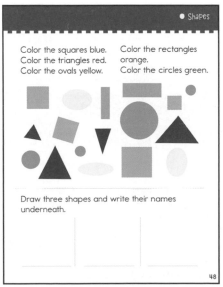

page 48

● Shapes

Color the squares blue.   Color the rectangles orange.
Color the triangles red.   Color the circles green.
Color the ovals yellow.

Draw three shapes and write their names underneath.

48

60

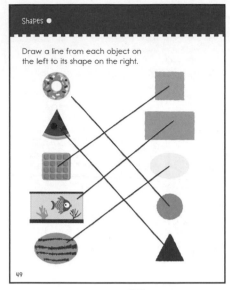

page 49

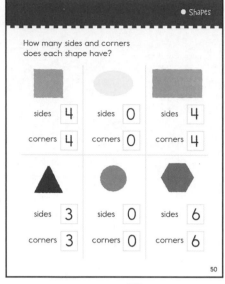

page 50

page 51

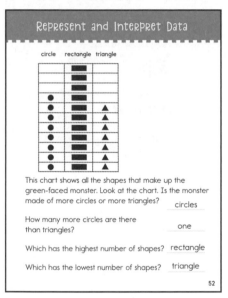

page 52

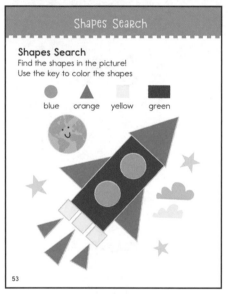

page 53

page 54

To My Grandson Ari —DAA

David A. Adler's First Grade Math Workbook copyright © 2022 by Holiday House Publishing, Inc.
Illustrations copyright © 2022 by Edward Miller III

Spot art from *Place Value* by David A. Adler, illustrations copyright © 2016 by Edward Miller III; from *Money Math* by David A. Adler, illustrations copyright © 2017 by Edward Miller III; and from *Telling Time* by David A. Adler, illustrations copyright © 2019 by Edward Miller III.

HOLIDAY HOUSE is registered in the U.S. Patent and Trademark Office.
Printed and bound in May 2022 at Toppan Leefung, DongGuan, China.
The artwork was created digitally.
www.holidayhouse.com
First Edition
1 3 5 7 9 10 8 6 4 2

ISBN: 978-0-8234-5314-6 (workbook)